BRAIN GAMES®

RETRO TRIVIA PUZZLES

Flash back to the '70s and '80s

pil

Publications International, Ltd.

Images from Shutterstock.com

Brain Games is a registered trademark of Publications International, Ltd.

Louis Weber, CEO
Publications International, Ltd.
8140 Lehigh Avenue
Morton Grove, IL 60053

Permission is never granted for commercial purposes.

ISBN: 978-1-64030-278-5

Manufactured in U.S.A.

8 7 6 5 4 3 2 1

1. Match each musical group to the film or TV show that inspired its name.

1) Duran Duran	A. The Wild One
2) T'Pau	B. Ferris Bueller's Day Off
3) Save Ferris	C. Barbarella
4) The Fratellis	D. Star Trek: The Original Series
5) Black Rebel Motorcycle Club	E. The Adventures of Tintin
6) Atreyu	F. The Goonies
7) Thompson Twins	G. The Neverending Story

2. What do all four of these famous people have in common?

(A) Larry Blyden

(B) Moss Hart

(C) Johnny Carson

(D) Groucho Marx

3. What was golfer Arnold Palmer's nickname?

(A) The Golden Bear

(B) The Great White Shark

(C) The Hawk

(D) The King

1. 1) C; 2) D; 3) B; 4) F; 5) A; 6) G; 7) E

Dr. Durand Durand, T'Pau, the Fratellis, Atreyu, and the Thompson Twins are all characters in their respective works. "Save Ferris" was a fundraising campaign, and the Black Rebels were—you guessed it—a motorcycle club.

2. They all hosted TV game shows.

3. D. The most popular golfer of all time, Arnie is known by millions of fans (dubbed "Arnie's Army") simply as "The King." If you've heard the other monikers but can't tie them to their owners, here you go: the Golden Bear is Jack Nicklaus, the Great White Shark is Greg Norman, and the Hawk was Ben Hogan.

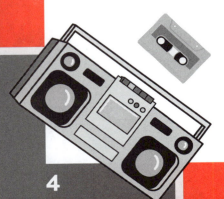

4. John Williams, winner of many Oscars, Grammys, Golden Globes, and Emmy awards, and composer of some of the most recognizable film scores in history, also composed the theme music for three of these four events. Which of the following did not at one time have a theme composed by Williams?

(A) Olympics

(B) Academy Awards show

(C) NBC Nightly News

(D) NBC Sunday Night Football

5. The vowels are missing from this classic TV show. What is it?

DLLS

6. How many astronauts have walked on the moon?

(A) 9

(B) 12

(C) 14

(D) 15

4. B. Fun fact: Williams was originally a jazz composer and musician. He has said he loved writing music for 2002's Catch Me If You Can because he got to return to his roots.

5. Dallas

6. B. Between July 20, 1969, and December 19, 1972, six Apollo missions landed on the moon. Altogether, 12 astronauts spent time on lunar soil.

7. The vowels are missing from this classic movie. What is it?

GRS

8. What color is Pac-Man?

9. Which of the following superstars got his start on TV, making guest appearances in Another World, Growing Pains, Dallas, and 21 Jump Street?

(A) Leonardo DiCaprio

(B) Johnny Depp

(C) Brad Pitt

(D) George Clooney

10. Halley's Comet last appeared in 1986. When is it scheduled to appear next?

(A) 2041

(B) 2048

(C) 2061

(D) 2087

7. Grease

8. Yellow

9. C. DiCaprio had a major role near the end of Growing Pains' run, and Depp was the main attraction on 21 Jump Street, but Pitt was a guest star on all those shows. He also appeared on Friends as a former classmate of Jennifer Aniston's Rachel. Were you aware that they used to be married in real life?

10. C. The comet is visible from Earth every 75 to 76 years as it orbits the Sun. American author Mark Twain was born two weeks after the comet's perihelion (when it's closest to the sun) in 1835, and he predicted he would live until the comet's return. He died April 21, 1910—the day after the comet's next perihelion.

11. At which well-known vacation destination did Richard Nixon deliver his infamous "I'm not a crook" speech?

(A) Camp David

(B) Mount Rushmore

(C) The Grand Canyon

(D) Walt Disney World

12. Complete the retro band name: The Swingin' Blue _____

(A) Sky

(B) Sea

(C) Bayou

(D) Jeans

13. Inky, Blinky, and Pinky are three of Pac-Man's four enemies. Who is the fourth?

(A) Clinky

(B) Clyde

(C) Dinky

(D) Steve

11. **D. On November 17, 1973, Richard Nixon delivered the "I'm not a crook" speech from The Contemporary Resort inside the Walt Disney World Resort. On that day, the sprawling theme park, having opened to the public just over two years prior, may not have been the happiest place on Earth.**

12. **D. Jeans**

13. **B. Clyde is the orange ghost. Blinky is red, Inky is blue, and Pinky is, well, pink.**

14. Which future TV star was pulled onstage to dance with Bruce Springsteen in the music video for "Dancing in the Dark"?

(A) Courteney Cox

(B) Calista Flockhart

(C) Teri Hatcher

(D) Sarah Jessica Parker

15. The vowels are missing from this classic movie. What is it?

MTBLLS

16. Which of the following doesn't belong, and why?

(A) Reggie Jackson

(B) George Brett

(C) Fred Lynn

(D) Earl Campbell

(E) Dave Winfield

14. **A. It looks like an impromptu performance, but in fact Cox was cast for the part by director Brian de Palma. On Springsteen's Born in the U.S.A. tour, however, the thrill of a lifetime was real: The Boss selected a young woman at random to be his dance partner at each concert.**

15. **Meatballs**

16. **D. Earl Campbell, because the others are baseball players.**

17. To protect a film's secrets, productions sometimes use a fake working title. Which of the following films went under the fake working title Blue Harvest?

(A) Superman II

(B) Return of the Jedi

(C) E.T.: The Extra-Terrestrial

(D) The Abyss

18. Which book uses exactly 50 different words?

19. Who is the first character to speak in the movie Star Wars, and what does that character say?

20. Which was the first song used to develop MP3s?

(A) Suzanne Vega's "Tom's Diner"

(B) The Moody Blues' "Nights in White Satin"

(C) Procol Harum's "A Whiter Shade of Pale"

(D) The Beatles' "Blackbird"

Answers from previous page:

17. B. The third Star Wars film also went through an actual name change. George Lucas, who initially called his third installment Revenge of the Jedi, decided that Jedis don't seek revenge and opted instead for Return of the Jedi. The sixth film's name, Revenge of the Sith, alludes to Jedi's original title. Speaking of allusions, the writers of The Simpsons gave their feature film debut the working title of Yellow Harvest as, what else, a joke.

18. Dr. Seuss's Green Eggs and Ham. Seuss's editor bet him he couldn't write a book using 50 words or less. Guess what? The editor lost.

19. C-3PO, the droid with the snazzy gold paint job, speaks first. He says to R2-D2, "Did you hear that?"

20. A. The theory behind the development of MP3s dates back to 1894 with the concept of auditory masking, or when tones block the sound of other tones. It only took them 100 years to figure it out.

21. Match the actor with his or her stage name.

1) Yul Brynner   A. Issur Demsky

2) Divine   B. Taidje Khan

3) Whoopi Goldberg   C. Joyce Frankenberg

4) Kirk Douglas   D. Caryn Johnson

5) Jane Seymour   E. Glenn Milstead

22. Complete the retro band name: _____ Alarm Clock

(A) Blueberry

(B) Loud

(C) Electric

(D) Strawberry

23. What do all four of these famous people have in common?

(A) Steve Allen

(B) Henry Kissinger

(C) John Denver

(D) John Anderson

21. 1) B; 2) E; 3) D; 4) A; 5) C.

22. D. Strawberry

23. They all wear (or wore) glasses.

24. True or False: Although common now, prior to the '70s very few World Series games were played at night.

25. True or False: Hugh Hefner saved the famous Hollywood sign by hosting a fund-raiser at the Playboy Mansion.

26. The James Bond series is famous for its gorgeous leading ladies. Can you match the Bond Girl with the movie in which she appeared?

1) The Man With the Golden Gun   A. Jinx Johnson

2) You Only Live Twice   B. Kissy Suzuki

3) Quantum of Solace   C. Mary Goodnight

4) Casino Royale   D. Strawberry Fields

5) Die Another Day   E. Vesper Lynd

27. The vowels are missing from this classic movie. What is it?

CDDSHCK

24. True: The first night game of the World Series didn't occur until 1971. More fans had televisions by this point, and MLB realized they could get more viewers if the games were on after people came home from work and school.

25. True. Hefner offered stars the chance to "adopt" the letters of the sign for $27,500 each, and started things off by adopting the Y himself. Actor Gene Autry bought an L, and rocker Alice Cooper saved an O. The rebuilt sign was unveiled in November 1978.

26. 1) C; 2) B; 3) D; 4) E; 5) A.

27. Caddyshack

28. Many famous rock 'n' roll bands went by different names before they made it big. Can you identify the former names of these bands?

1) The Beatles   A. Feedback; The Hype

2) Journey   B. Golden Gate Rhythm Section

3) KISS   C. The Pendletones

4) The Rolling Stones   D. Satan's Jesters

5) U2   E. Wicked Lester

29. Who scored the winning goal for the U.S. men's hockey team in the "Miracle on Ice" game against the Soviet Union in the 1980 Olympics?

(A) Mike Eruzione

(B) Mark Johnson

(C) Rob McClanahan

(D) Dave Silk

30. Which is the real first name of "Sparky" Anderson?

(A) Sparky

(B) Andrew

(C) George

(D) Harry

28. 1) C; 2) B; 3) E; 4) D; 5) A.

29. A. Eruzione was the team captain. His winning goal—one of the most played highlights in American sports—was voted the greatest highlight of all time by ESPN viewers in 2008.

30. C. George

31. The Turbo PC, the first personal computer, was designed by what manufacturer in 1985?

(A) Acer

(B) Packard Bell

(C) Dell

(D) Gateway

32. What was the original name of the Beatles?

(A) The Quarrymen

(B) The Birdmen

(C) The London Boys Club

(D) The Longhairs

33. True or False: In the original script for E.T.: The Extra-Terrestrial, the adorable alien dies.

34. By which name was Will Smith known during his early rap career?

31. C. Founder Michael Dell dropped out of college to found PCs Limited, which would quickly become Dell Computer Corporation, and eventually Dell Inc. The Turbo PC sold for $795, and after one year in business, Michael Dell's company had grossed more than $73 million. Stay in school, shmay in school.

32. A.

33. True. Children hated the original ending, so director Steven Spielberg changed the script so the lovable E.T. could go back home.

34. The Fresh Prince. He later starred on the TV show The Fresh Prince of Bel-Air (1990–96). At the time, few people would have predicted that the rapper would eventually be Oscar-nominated (Ali, 2001, and The Pursuit of Happyness, 2006).

35. **What was the first video ever played on MTV?**

(A) "Beat It," Michael Jackson

(B) "Money for Nothing," Dire Straits

(C) "Paradise by the Dashboard Light," Meat Loaf

(D) "Video Killed the Radio Star," The Buggles

36. **Which is the real first name of "Bo" Jackson?**

(A) Beau

(B) Robert

(C) Michael

(D) Vincent

37. **In Star Wars, what is the name of Han Solo's spacecraft?**

(A) Apollo

(B) Enterprise

(C) Millennium Falcon

(D) Voyager

35. D. At midnight on August 1, 1981, MTV launched with the airing of the music video of the Buggles' 1979 debut single. Irony at its finest.

36. D. Vincent

37. C. The Falcon's design was allegedly inspired by a hamburger, with the cockpit being an olive on the side. Mmmm-mm. Hungry?

38. True or False: The Barbie doll first appeared in an astronaut uniform to commemorate Sally Ride's 1983 space shuttle mission, the first undertaken by an American woman.

39. The vowels are missing from this classic movie. What is it?

RPLN

40. The vowels are missing from this classic TV show. What is it?

BNNZ

41. What do all four of these famous people have in common?

A. Alan Alda

B. Larry Hagman

C. Elizabeth Montgomery

D. Mia Farrow

38. **False. Barbie got her astronaut on in 1965, nearly 20 years before Ride did it. Was it prescience or optimism? Neither. Soviet cosmonaut Valentina Tereshkova took a space ride June 16, 1963—a full 20 years before Ride became the first American woman to duplicate the feat.**

39. **Airplane**

40. **Bonanza**

41. **They are all offspring of famous people.**

42. In what year does the 1988 drama Eight Men Out take place?

(A) 1901

(B) 1909

(C) 1919

(D) 1925

43. Complete the retro band name: ? and the _____

(A) Punctuations

(B) Bohemians

(C) Mysterians

(D) Interrogations

44. What's the full name of Wizard of Oz author L. Frank Baum?

(A) Lawrence

(B) Lyon

(C) Lyman

(D) Leonard

42. **C. The film tells the story of the 1919 Black Sox scandal, when eight Chicago White Sox players deliberately threw the World Series to benefit gamblers.**

43. **C. Mysterians**

44. **C. Lyman**

45. Sequels sometimes take a while to show up. Match each original film to its sequel.

1) Chinatown	A. Staying Alive
2) The Hustler	B. Gator
3) White Lightning	C. From Russia with Love
4) Saturday Night Fever	D. The Two Jakes
5) Dirty Harry	E. Magnum Force
6) Dr. No	F. The Color of Money

46. How many stars of the 1987 sci-fi film Predator went on to become state governors?

47. Who famously said, "That's one small step for a man, one giant leap for mankind"?

(A) Buzz Aldrin

(B) Neil Armstrong

(C) John Glenn

(D) Buzz Lightyear

45. 1) D; 2) F; 3) B; 4) A; 5) E; 6) C

The biggest gap between sequels on this list is between **The Hustler** and **The Color of Money** at 25 years. As for the shortest, **Dr. No** and **From Russia with Love** came out in 1962 and 1963 respectively. People couldn't get enough James Bond.

46. Two. Body-builder-turned-movie-star Arnold Schwarzenegger went on to become the Governator of California; professional-wrestler-turned-conspiracy-theorist Jesse "The Body" Ventura went on to become governor of Minnesota. Minnesotans must like their politicians good and famous.

47. B. Armstrong was the first man to walk on the moon. Later that year, Apollo 12 astronaut Pete Conrad, shortest member of his astronaut corps, landed on the Moon, jumped down from his lunar module, and said, "Whoopie! That may have been a small one for Neil, but it's a long one for me."

48. Kevin Costner – who has quite a few baseball movies in his resume – plays the part of Crash Davis in 1988's Bull Durham. But who was originally tapped for the part?

(A) Bruce Willis

(B) Kurt Russell

(C) Dennis Quaid

(D) Gary Sinise

49. How many different dogs played the title role of the television show Lassie?

50. The vowels are missing from this classic TV show. What is it?

QNCY

51. Who is the only president never to have won a general election?

48. B. Russell helped writer Ron Shelton develop the script, and was reportedly quite impressed with the final choice of Costner for the part of Crash.

49. In its 20-year run, nine different collies helped extricate Timmy and other kids from perilous situations involving bodies of water, cliffs, quicksand, and mine shafts—though never from a well.

50. Quincy

51. Gerald Ford. Ford was nominated for and ultimately became vice president when Spiro Agnew resigned in 1973. After President Richard Nixon resigned in 1974, Ford became president. In 1976, he narrowly defeated Ronald Reagan for the Republican nomination for president but eventually lost to Jimmy Carter.

52. What do all four of these famous people have in common?

A. Cesar Romero

B. Eartha Kitt

C. Vincent Price

D. Otto Preminger

53. Who was the inspiration for the dude in Aerosmith's "Dude (Looks Like a Lady)"?

(A) Vince Neil (Mötley Crüe)

(B) Jon Bon Jovi (Bon Jovi)

(C) Dee Snider (Twisted Sister)

(D) Sebastian Bach (Skid Row)

54. In Roald Dahl's children's book of the same name, to what does The BFG refer?

(A) Belly Flop Gang

(B) Best Friends Guild

(C) Brain Freeze Gulp

(D) Big Friendly Giant

52. They all played criminals on Batman.

53. A. The song was released in 1987 at the height of the "hair bands," but 25 years before the manbun. We're due for a rerelease.

54. D. Standing 24 feet tall, the BFG's main job was to deliver good dreams to children. He first appeared in Dahl's Danny, the Champion of the World. Too bad he didn't show up in Dahl's James Bond script You Only Live Twice.

55. **Which of the following doesn't belong, and why?**

(A) Peter Pan

(B) Charlie Brown

(C) Rudolph the Reindeer

(D) Rocky the Flying Squirrel

(E) Superman

56. **Which teams played in the first Super Bowl?**

(A) Green Bay Packers and Oakland Raiders

(B) Green Bay Packers and Kansas City Chiefs

(C) Baltimore Colts and New York Jets

(D) Minnesota Vikings and Kansas City Chiefs

57. **Which of these rockers is the youngest?**

(A) Frank Zappa

(B) Brian Auger

(C) Roy Orbison

(D) Eric Clapton

55. B. Charlie Brown, because the others can fly.

56. B. The first Super Bowl, called the AFL–NFL World Championship Game, was played in February 1967. The Green Bay Packers beat the Kansas City Chiefs 35–10.

57. C.

58. True or False: In Friday the 13th Part II, Jason Voorhees' mask was based on a 1950s Detroit Red Wings goalie mask.

59. Star Trek has had many incarnations on television, including 2017's Discovery. Which run had the most episodes?

(A) The Original Series

(B) The Next Generation

(C) Deep Space Nine

(D) Voyager

(E) Enterprise

60. What was the original name of the Nike corporation?

(A) Apollo Sports

(B) Blue Ribbon Sports

(C) Gold Medal Sports

(D) Olympia Sports

58. False, but not for the reason you think. It was based on goaltender Terry Sawchuck's mask from the Red Wings—but Jason didn't wear it until Friday the 13th Part III.

59. B. It was close, but The Next Generation aired 178 episodes, plus four theatrical films. Deep Space Nine aired 176, Voyager aired 172, and Enterprise aired 98. Star Trek: The Original Series had only 79 episodes, but it did get four spin-off series, plus eight movies (and counting). Captain Kirk for the win!

60. B. In 1971 the founders of the small sports-shoe business Blue Ribbon Sports in Beaverton, Oregon, were searching for a catchy, energetic company name. They settled on Nike, the name of the Greek goddess of victory. And victorious they were: Nike is now the largest sportswear manufacturer in the world.

61. Which comedian famously riffed about the "Seven Words You Can Never Say on Television" way back in 1972?

(A) Bill Cosby

(B) Sam Kinison

(C) Richard Pryor

(D) George Carlin

62. What do the initials A. A. stand for in children's book author A. A. Milne's name?

(A) Alan Alexander

(B) Alex Axel

(C) Abbot Alexander

(D) Albert Alphonse

63. The 1974 World Heavyweight Championship boxing match in Zaire between George Foreman and Muhammad Ali was known by what name?

61. D. These days, you can actually say some of the words on broadcast TV or basic cable, and all bets are off on premium cable. But we're still not saying any of them here.

62. A. Alan Alexander

63. "The Rumble in the Jungle." The bout was stopped in the eighth round, with Ali handing Foreman his first-ever defeat.

64. How many actors did it take to portray Darth Vader in Star Wars?

65. The vowels are missing from this classic TV show. What is it?

TX

66. Can you name the five original MTV VJs?

67. Ozzy Osbourne became famous with which heavy metal band?

(A) AC/DC

(B) Black Sabbath

(C) Iron Maiden

(D) Judas Priest

64. Four. James Earl Jones provided Vader's deep, booming voice; David Prowse played the villain's body; Sebastian Shaw played the unmasked face; and sound designer Ben Burtt provided the dark lord's infamous breathing effect.

65. Taxi

66. Alan Hunter, Mark Goodman, Nina Blackwood, Martha Quinn, and J. J. Jackson.

67. B. B is for Black Sabbath, but it's also for bat—as in the bat whose head Ozzy legendarily bit off when a fan tossed it onto the stage at a 1982 concert.

68. Which is the real first name of "Yogi" Berra?

(A) Boo-Boo

(B) Barry

(C) James

(D) Lawrence

69. Ozzy Osbourne was famously banned from the city of San Antonio for a decade. What did he do to earn his banishment?

(A) Bit the head off a live bat in a concert there

(B) Gave a lewd, nude public performance

(C) Urinated on the Alamo

(D) Started a riot

70. Which band did not feature legendary guitarist Eric Clapton? You can skim one answer right off the top.

(A) The Yardbirds

(B) Traffic

(C) Cream

(D) Derek and the Dominos

68. D. Lawrence

69. C. Osbourne acted in a drunken stupor, but later made up with the city by donating $20,000 to the Daughters of the Republic of Texas to help restore the national landmark. We bet Ozzy doesn't have any trouble remembering the Alamo these days!

70. B. Steve Winwood, who formed Traffic with three friends, later went on to form the band Blind Faith with Clapton.

71. Complete the retro band name: The Flamin' _____

(A) Arrows

(B) Players

(C) Grooves

(D) Guitars

72. The vowels are missing from this classic movie. What is it?

RCK

73. An interrobang is made by combining what two punctuation marks?

(A) ! and ?

(B) > and <

(C)) and (

(D) : and %

74. The vowels are missing from this classic TV show. What is it?

LC

71. C. Grooves

72. Rocky

73. A. Invented in 1962 by advertiser Martin Spektor, the combination expresses surprise in a question. Through the early 1970s, the key could be found on typewriters or as an add-on, but the fad faded away like a forgotten pet rock. That's great, right?!

74. Alice

75. What famous world event happened on November 9, 1989?

(A) The TV show Seinfeld premiered

(B) The Berlin Wall fell

(C) Ayatollah Khomeini died

(D) Tiananmen Square massacre occurred

76. Complete the retro band name: We _____

(A) Willie Winkies

(B) Are Family

(C) Five

(D) Wees

77. Which is the real first name of "Catfish" Hunter?

(A) Rod

(B) James

(C) Gil

(D) Tab

75. B. What a big year in history 1989 happened to be. All of the events above occurred in 1989, but the toppling of the Berlin Wall and reunification of Germany began on November 9. British Prime Minister Margaret Thatcher begged Soviet President Mikhail Gorbachev not to let it happen because she feared the worst for Europe.

76. C. Five

77. B. James

78. Finish the title. Close Encounters of the Third...

(A) Reich

(B) Kind

(C) Base

(D) Wave

79. What do all four of these famous figures have in common?

A. Pamela North

B. Travis McGee

C. Michael Shayne

D. Pete Chambers

80. Which famous athlete not-so-humbly claimed, "When you are as great as I am, it's hard to be humble"?

(A) Muhammad Ali

(B) Charles Barkley

(C) Reggie Jackson

(D) Babe Ruth

78. B. Kind

79. They are all fictional detectives.

80. A. Not only could the champion boxer float like a butterfly and sting like a bee, but he was also a champion boaster.

81. What 1970s film was the first to feature a computer-generated title sequence?

(A) Jaws 2

(B) Revenge of the Pink Panther

(C) Grease

(D) Superman

82. What do all four of these famous people have in common?

A. Ava Gardner

B. Mia Farrow

C. Barbara Marx

D. Nancy Barbato

83. The vowels are missing from this classic movie. What is it?

SPRMN

84. What does the ZIP in ZIP code stand for?

Answers from previous page:

81. D. Superman became the first of many films to use computer animation in its opening sequence. Released in 1978, Superman's production preceded a boom in digital filmmaking by only a few years (the CGI-heavy Tron was released in 1982). As such, the film's creative team had to manufacture a 70-foot scale model of the Golden Gate Bridge, as well as one for the Hoover Dam.

82. They were all married to Frank Sinatra.

83. Superman

84. Zoning Improvement Plan. The United States Postal Service established this system in 1963.

85. **Which of the following doesn't belong, and why?**

(A) Walter Cronkite

(B) John Chancellor

(C) John Dean

(D) David Brinkley

(E) Tom Brokaw

86. **Saturday Night Live premiered on October 11, 1975. Who was its first-ever celebrity host?**

(A) Desi Arnaz

(B) Candice Bergen

(C) George Carlin

(D) Bob Newhart

87. **In how many movies did John Wayne die?**

88. **The vowels are missing from this classic movie. What is it?**

RTHQK

85. c) John Dean, because the others are newscasters.

86. C. Unlike today's guest hosts, who appear in most of the show's sketches, Carlin only appeared onstage to perform stand-up comedy and introduce the musical guests.

87. Seven: Reap the Wild Wind, The Fighting Seabees, Wake of the Red Witch, Sands of Iwo Jima, The Alamo, The Cowboys, and The Shootist.

88. Earthquake

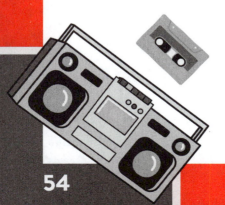

89. Who was the first woman to serve on the U.S. Supreme Court?

(A) Ruth Bader Ginsburg

(B) Sonia Sotomayor

(C) Elena Kagan

(D) Sandra Day O'Connor

90. The vowels are missing from this classic movie. What is it?

JWS

91. Which of these players won World Series MVP at just 21?

(A) Lew Burdette

(B) Sandy Koufax

(C) Bret Saberhagen

(D) Johnny Bench

92. The vowels are missing from this classic movie. What is it?

CNDRLL

Answers from previous page:

89. **D. Justice O'Connor was nominated by president Reagan in 1981 and served until 2006. One of Justice O'Connor's challenges on the High Court was finding where to go (and we don't mean "getting directions"). Since there had never been a woman on the Supreme Court before, there were no nearby women's restroom facilities.**

90. **Jaws**

91. **C. Saberhagen, who pitched in the 1985 World Series for the Kansas City Royals, was 21 years, six months, 16 days old when he won the award. He pitched two complete games, including a shutout, and helped the Royals win the championship. He won the American League Cy Young Award the same year.**

92. **Cinderella**

93. Whose face has appeared on the cover of Rolling Stone magazine more than anyone else's?

(A) Bob Dylan

(B) Eric Clapton

(C) Tiny Tim

(D) John Lennon

94. Who was Will Smith's hip-hop collaborator (and occasional TV friend)?

95. Which piano-playing entertainer earned the nicknames "Mr. Showmanship" and "The Glitter Man"?

(A) Stevie Wonder

(B) Liberace

(C) Elton John

(D) Billy Joel

96. How many golf balls are on the moon?

93. C.

94. DJ Jazzy Jeff

95. B. Liberace's legendary bedazzled pianos were no match for his wardrobe, which included such gems as a blue fox cape that trailed 16 feet behind him and a King Neptune costume that weighed 200 pounds.

96. Two. Apollo 14 astronaut Alan Shepard hit both in 1971. And the spectacle wouldn't have been complete without advice from the peanut gallery: Mission Control offered Shepard advice on his stance, which was somewhat hampered by his space suit.

97. What was rock music's first "supergroup" —a musical act in which all of the members had already had successful careers as part of a band or solo act?

(A) Cream

(B) Crosby, Stills & Nash

(C) Emerson, Lake & Palmer

(D) Traveling Wilburys

98. Which CD was the first one manufactured in the U.S.?

(A) Billy Joel's 52nd Street

(B) Bruce Springsteen's Born in the U.S.A.

(C) Cyndi Lauper's She's So Unusual

(D) Blondie's The Hunter

99. Complete the retro band name: Count ___

(A) Down

(B) Over

(C) Five

(D) This

97. A. Eric Clapton, Jack Bruce, and Ginger Baker were stars in their own right before they formed Cream, which released its first album in 1967. Unfortunately, the relationship soured in only two years.

98. B. Joel's 1978 album was the first to be available for sale on CD in Japan in 1982, but Springsteen's most iconic album was aptly named—it was the first to be made in the U.S.A. starting in September 1984.

99. C. Five

100. Richard Bachman is the alter ego of which famous author?

(A) Stephen King

(B) John Grisham

(C) Tom Wolfe

(D) John Updike

101. Who directed the 1984 drama The Natural?

(A) Bennett Miller

(B) Barry Levinson

(C) Phil Alden Robinson

(D) Sam Raimi

102. In the Back to the Future franchise, at what speed is the DeLorean time machine activated?

(A) 78 mph

(B) 88 mph

(C) 98 mph

(D) 108 mph

100. A. King chose the name Richard after crime novelist Donald E. Westlake's pseudonym, Richard Stark, and Bachman for the band Bachman-Turner Overdrive. He started writing under the pen name to test whether it was his talent or his name that sold books. He wrote four novels (Rage, The Long Walk, Roadwork, and The Running Man) before being discovered. King continues to reference his most lifelike creation to this day.

101. B. Levinson is also known for directing Diner, Rain Man, Toys, and Good Morning, Vietnam.

102. B. Hello? McFly? Is anybody home? Of course you knew that the flux capacitor kicks into gear at 88 miles per hour.

103. Complete the retro band name: Tower of ___

(A) London

(B) Pisa

(C) Power

(D) Babel

104. The vowels are missing from this classic TV show. What is it?

FRDYS

105. Colonel Sanders (of KFC fame) was named an honorary Kentucky Colonel by the state's governor, and he's in good company. Which of these figures was not made an honorary Kentucky Colonel?

(A) Muhammad Ali

(B) Pope John Paul II

(C) Al Gore

(D) Whoopi Goldberg

103. C. Power

104. Fridays

105. C. It's hard to imagine this group sitting on the veranda drinking mint juleps together.

106. Which of the following doesn't belong, and why?

(A) Elton John

(B) Mick Jagger

(C) Bruce Hornsby

(D) Bill Murray

(E) Paul M

107. Complete the retro band name: Stone The _____

(A) Heretics

(B) Quarrymen

(C) Crows

(D) Family

108. Complete the retro band name: Vanilla _____

(A) Ice Cream

(B) Extract

(C) Manila

(C) Fudge

106. D. Bill Murray, because the others are singers. His karaoke turn in Lost in Translation only almost counts.

107. C. Crows

108. D. Fudge

109. What are the names of the two old men who sit in the balcony on The Muppet Show?

(A) Aspin and Ludsthorp

(B) Chilton and Gerard

(C) Hawkins and Nigel

(D) Waldorf and Statler

110. Which country singer is known as the Man in Black?

(A) Clint Black

(B) Garth Brooks

(C) Johnny Cash

(D) Hank Williams

111. The vowels are missing from this classic movie. What is it?

LN

109. D. The ornery octogenarians enjoy heckling the other Muppets from the best seats in the house. Their names are based on hotels in New York: the Waldorf–Astoria and the Statler Hilton.

110. C. Cash has been inducted into the Country Music Hall of Fame, the Rock and Roll Hall of Fame, the Gospel Music Hall of Fame, and the Rockabilly Hall of Fame.

111. Alien

112. As Apple developed the Power Mac 7100 in the early 1990s, it used the name of a famous astronomer as a code name. Who was the astronomer?

(A) Albert Einstein

(B) Edwin Hubble

(C) Carl Sagan

(D) Clyde Tombaugh

113. Complete the retro band name: Van Der Graff _____

(A) Generator

(B) Zeppelin

(C) Morrison

(D) Boys

114. Which of the following doesn't belong, and why?

(A) Kermit

(B) Bert

(C) Ernie

(D) Alvin

(E) Oscar

112. **C. Sagan sued the company over the use of his name (and lost), but Apple decided to change the code name anyway, to "BHA." What did BHA stand for, you ask? "Butt-head astronomer."**

113. **A. Generator**

114. **D. Alvin, because the others are Muppets.**

115. Who was the director of the FBI for almost half of the 20th century?

(A) Winston Churchill

(B) Allen Dulles

(C) J. Edgar Hoover

(D) Howard Hughes

116. Which actress played Gertie in the movie E.T. the Extra-Terrestrial?

(A) Drew Barrymore

(B) Cameron Diaz

(C) Gwyneth Paltrow

(D) Reese Witherspoon

117. Which war do the movies Apocalypse Now, Full Metal Jacket, Hamburger Hill, and Platoon depict?

(A) Vietnam War

(B) Korean War

(C) Spanish Civil War

(D) Crimean War

115. C. Hoover was appointed in 1924 and held the position until his death in 1972. He established the world's largest fingerprint file, a scientific detection lab, and the FBI National Academy, among many other accomplishments. He also used the organization's secret files to his benefit by blackmailing politicians to secure his powerful position. Leonardo DiCaprio portrayed Hoover in the 2011 movie J. Edgar (and Howard Hughes in 2004's The Aviator).

116. A. Barrymore was just seven years old when she starred in the blockbuster movie.

117. A. Including Good Morning, Vietnam would have made it too easy.

118. Complete the retro band name: 1910 _____ Company

(A) Bubblegum

(B) Fruitcake

(C) Fruitcup

(D) Fruitgum

119. Complete the retro band name: Ten Years _____

(A) Behind

(B) After

(C) Later

(D) Too Late

120. Finish the title. The Hills Have_____

(A) Peaks

(B) Billies

(C) Eyes

(D) Brothers

118. D. Fruitgum

119. B. After

120. C. Eyes

121. **Which creepy actor also penned a gourmet cookbook?**

(A) Boris Karlov

(B) Bela Lugosi

(C) Willem Dafoe

(D) Vincent Price

122. **What is the name for little LEGO people?**

(A) Figurines

(B) Action figures

(C) Minifigs

(D) Fig Newtons

123. **The late 1970s TV show Shields and Yarnell was a showcase for what performance art?**

(A) Break dance

(B) Sculpture

(C) Mime

(D) Yarn bombing

124. True or False: **Bob Newhart never won an Emmy for his role in Newhart.**

121. D. Long before he did the voiceover for Michael Jackson's Thriller, Price and his wife, Mary, penned the terrifyingly good A Treasury of Great Recipes (1965).

122. C. Short for "minifigures," minifigs came on the LEGO scene in 1974. At that time, they had no arms—an oversight that has thankfully been rectified.

123. C. Mimes Robert Shields and Lorene Yarnell were married in a mime wedding in Union Square and went on to win an Emmy for their television program.

124. True: Surprisingly, the hilarious Newhart never won an Emmy for any of his regular television work. He finally won an Emmy in 2013 for Outstanding Guest Actor in a Comedy Series for his role as Professor Proton on the sitcom The Big Bang Theory.

125. What is the real first name of Indiana Jones?

(A) Max

(B) Henry

(C) Frank

(D) Joe

126. Which former Beatle was the first person to be featured on the cover of Rolling Stone?

(A) George Harrison

(B) Paul McCartney

(C) John Lennon

(D) Ringo Starr

127. Brat Pack movies The Breakfast Club, Ferris Bueller's Day Off, and Sixteen Candles (all directed by John Hughes) were set in the suburbs of which metropolis?

(A) Boston

(B) Chicago

(C) Los Angeles

(D) Philadelphia

125. B. The nickname came from Jones's childhood dog (who was in turn named for a dog owned by series creator George Lucas).

126. C. No, it wasn't the naked picture with Yoko Ono—in 1967, Lennon was featured in a still from the film How I Won the War. All told, Lennon was featured on the cover of three of the first ten issues of Rolling Stone.

127. B. It seems there was no place like home for Hughes, who grew up in Northbrook, Illinois, a suburb of Chicago.

128. What do Homer Simpson and Elvis Presley have in common?

129. The vowels are missing from this classic TV show. What is it?

BNSN

130. Can you name the song each of these lyrics comes from?

A. "Thunderbolt and lightning, very, very frightening."

B. "A singer in a smoky room, a smell of wine and cheap perfume."

C. "Hands, touching hands, reaching out, touching me, touching you."

D. "Well, I know that you're in love with him, 'cause I saw you dancin' in the gym."

E. "You start to scream, but terror takes the sound before you make it."

128. **They both have daughters named Lisa Marie.**

129. **Benson**

130. **A. "Bohemian Rhapsody" (Queen);**

B. "Don't Stop Believin'" (Journey);

C. "Sweet Caroline" (Neil Diamond);

D. "American Pie" (Don McLean);

E. "Thriller" (Michael Jackson).

131. Which of the following doesn't belong, and why?

(A) Marmaduke

(B) Bullwinkle

(C) Sylvester

(D) Scooby-Doo

(E) Popeye

132. Complete the retro band name: Curved _____

(A) Hair

(B) Road

(C) Air

(D) Grades

133. Which of these musical acts turned down the chance to perform at the 1969 Woodstock Music and Art Festival?

(A) The Grateful Dead

(B) Sly & the Family Stone

(C) Jethro Tull

(D) Jefferson Airplane

131. E. Popeye, because the others are animals.

132. C. Air

133. C. In an interview, front man Ian Anderson cited his aversion to hippies and spontaneous outdoor nudity as reasons for turning down the gig.

134. The first commercially sold home video-game console was:

(A) RCA Studio II

(B) Coleco Telstar

(C) Magnavox Odyssey

(D) Atari Pong

135. Finish the title. In the Heat of the...

(A) Hot Tub

(B) Beat

(C) Day

(D) Night

136. What retro name did the core group of friends use to refer to themselves on the series Buffy the Vampire Slayer (1997–2003)?

(A) The Badanovs

(B) The Felix Faith

(C) The Scooby Gang

(D) The Underdog Squad

134. C. Released three years before Atari's home version of Pong, the Odyssey was the only thing going in 1972. Though the Odyssey did not feature Pong's familiar sounds, players could play tennis with a pair of rotating paddles. Magnavox tried suing Atari for copyright infringement; the Odyssey's inventor went on to create Simon, the popular electronic game, in 1978.

135. D. Night

136. C. Buffy, Willow, Xander, and Giles formed the core of the Scooby Gang, or the Scoobies. The spooky goings-on in Sunnydale, California, influenced today's vampire, werewolf, and supernatural craze.

137. What's the full name of blues legend B. B. King?

(A) Big Bopper

(B) Big Boy

(C) Riley B.

(D) Baby Blue

138. Which celebrity was Al Gore's college roommate at Harvard?

(A) Billy Crystal

(B) Tommy Lee Jones

(C) Steven Spielberg

(D) Henry Winkler

139. Which of the following actors from the Star Wars film series was a step-cousin to Ian Fleming, author of the James Bond novels?

(A) Alec Guinness (Obi-Wan Kenobi)

(B) Anthony Daniels (C-3PO)

(C) Liam Neeson (Qui-Gon Jinn)

(D) Christopher Lee (Count Dooku)

137. C. Riley B., confusingly. Call it a misnicknomer.

138. B. Can you imagine the former vice president and Agent K from Men in Black hanging out between classes? Doesn't seem too far-fetched.

139. D. Lee's mother married into Fleming's family, but it was his acting that got him a part as the James Bond villain Scaramanga in The Man with the Golden Gun, right? Maybe. Lee was Fleming's regular golf partner after all. Do you think he ever golfed with George Lucas?

140. **Which two players have each hit a record five home runs in a single World Series?**

(A) David Ortiz, Chase Utley

(B) Barry Bonds, David Ortiz

(C) Reggie Jackson, Barry Bonds

(D) Reggie Jackson, Chase Utley

141. **Who was the group Jethro Tull named after?**

(A) the mayor of Casterbridge

(B) the inventor of vermouth

(C) a character from The Wizard of Oz

(D) the 17th-century inventor of the seed drill

142. **What is the only X-rated movie ever to win an Academy Award for Best Picture?**

143. **Which MLB team is represented in the 1989 film Major League?**

(A) Cincinnati Reds

(B) Philadelphia Phillies

(C) Chicago Cubs

(D) Cleveland Indians

140. D. Jackson hit five home runs during the 1977 World Series, earning him his nickname, "Mr. October." Thirty-two years later, Utley did the same in the 2009 series.

141. D.

142. Midnight Cowboy. The movie, starring Dustin Hoffman and Jon Voight, took home the prize in 1969. Because of the growing stigma associated with X ratings, the film's rating was changed to R in 1971 without anything being changed or removed.

143. D. In the movie, the owner of the Indians, Rachel Phelps (played by Margaret Whitton), hires terrible players so the team will lose and she can move them to Miami. Of course, her plot ends up backfiring in hilarious ways!

144. Which of the following doesn't belong, and why?

(A) John Glenn

(B) Gary Powers

(C) Neil Armstrong

(D) John Young

(E) Buzz Aldrin

145. Two players are tied for the most runs scored in a single World Series: Reggie Jackson, and who else?

(A) Albert Pujols

(B) Jim Thome

(C) Paul Molitor

(D) Mickey Mantle

146. Which of the following doesn't belong, and why?

(A) Richard Burton

(B) Eddie Fisher

(C) Montgomery Clift

(D) Michael Wilding

(E) Michael Todd

Answers from previous page:

144. B. Gary Powers, because the others are astronauts.

145. C. Both players scored 10 runs – Jackson in the 1977 World Series for the New York Yankees, and Molitor in the 1993 series for the Toronto Blue Jays.

146. C. Montgomery Clift, because the others are Liz Taylor's ex-husbands.

147. **What do all four of these famous people have in common?**

A. Gwen Verdon

B. Emily Dickinson

C. Lucille Ball

D. Thomas Jefferson

148. **Who played Indiana Jones's father in Indiana Jones and the Temple of Doom?**

(A) Sean Connery

(B) James Garner

(C) Gene Hackman

(D) Peter O'Toole

149. The vowels are missing from this classic TV show. What is it?

TMRRW

147. They are all redheads.

148. A. Yep, James Bond himself was also Indy's dad. Director Steven Spielberg thought Connery was an obvious choice for the role, as Bond was an inspiration for Indiana's character.

149. Tomorrow

150. What do all four of these famous figures have in common?

A. Will Scarlet

B. John Little

C. Arthur-a-Bland

D. Will Stutely

151. Where was the world's first Starbucks?

(A) Portland, Oregon

(B) San Francisco, California

(C) Seattle, Washington

(D) Vancouver, Canada

152. The Woodstock Music and Art Festival was held August 15–18, 1969, not in Woodstock but in Bethel, New York, 40 miles away. Woodstock was supposed to host the festival, but when rumors spread that attendance could reach a million people, the city backed out. Dairy farmer Max Yasgur saved the concert by hosting it in a field at his farm. What crop was growing in that field?

(A) Alfalfa

(B) Cabbage

(C) Corn

(D) Marijuana

150. They are all members of Robin Hood's gang.

151. C. Although today it may seem like there's a Starbucks on every corner, there was a time when you would have had to travel to Seattle to get your morning fix. When it opened in 1971, the store didn't even sell coffee by the cup; it sold small batches of fresh-roasted coffee.

152. A. Alfalfa is the answer, but the free-spirited flower children who attended the concert might have preferred one of the other options.

153. What's the full name of science fiction pioneer H. G. Wells?

(A) Howard Glenn

(B) Harry Gary

(C) Hoppin Gater

(D) Herbert George

154. Clint Eastwood was far from the studio's first choice to "make their day" as Dirty Harry. Which of these actors was not offered the role before Eastwood?

(A) Frank Sinatra

(B) John Wayne

(C) Robert Redford

(D) Paul Newman

155. The vowels are missing from this classic TV show. What is it?

TH JFFRSNS

153. D. Herbert George

154. C. When Eastwood was finally offered the role, he felt very lucky indeed.

155. The Jeffersons

156. Which of these sweet treats has not been featured as a main ingredient in a breakfast cereal?

(A) AirHeads

(B) Ice cream

(C) Raisinets

(D) Nerds candy

157. What's the full name of novelist P. D. James?

(A) Phyllis Dorothy

(B) Patricia Darlene

(C) Paula Deborah

(D) Pansy Daffodil

158. The vowels are missing from this classic TV show. What is it?

GNSMK

156. C. Although sugar-happy tykes everywhere might think Raisin Bran could be improved by coating the raisins with chocolate, no such cereal has been created . . . yet. Cap'n Crunch's AirHeads Berries was produced by Quaker in 2003. In 1965 Kellogg's introduced Kream Krunch, which was filled with bits of freeze-dried ice cream. And the tangy flavor of Nerds candy was re-created in Nerds Cereal in the mid-1980s, with Ralston cleverly dividing the cereal box in half to feature a different flavor in each compartment, just like the candy box.

157. A. It's no mystery that her name is Phyllis Dorothy.

158. Gunsmoke

159. True or False: Michael Jackson's "Thriller" video was nominated for an Academy Award.

160. Which part of the Statue of Liberty was retired and replaced in 1984?

161. What's the full name of fictional Dallas landowner J. R. Ewing, Jr.?

(A) Just Right

(B) James Randolph

(C) Jack Roger

(D) John Ross

162. Which Oscar-nominated actor is rumored to have hated the '80s TV show he starred on so much that he lit his underwear on fire in an attempt to get fired?

(A) George Clooney

(B) Johnny Depp

(C) Tom Hanks

(D) Will Smith

159. False. It wasn't nominated, but producers made sure it was eligible by giving it a one-week theatrical release in 1983, opening for the Disney movie Fantasia. Parents weren't too thrilled about their toddlers getting an eyeful of zombie action, but that was only because they hadn't yet had to sit through 2017's Olaf's Frozen Adventure.

160. The current torch is actually the second for Lady Liberty. The first was removed in 1984 and can be seen up close and personal on display in the Pedestal lobby.

161. D. Who Shot John Ross?

162. B. When Depp joined the cast of 21 Jump Street in 1987, he did so believing it would be for only one season. When the show became a hit, he was stuck. Eager to be taken more seriously, Depp got creative in trying to escape his contract, but it took four long seasons before he was finally free to leave. He apparently got over his distaste for the role, however, and good-naturedly made a cameo in the 2012 movie based on the series.

163. How many national championships did UCLA win in the John Wooden coaching era?

(A) 7

(B) 8

(C) 9

(D) 10

164. Who made the winning shot in North Carolina's 1982 NCAA title game victory over Georgetown?

(A) Michael Jordan

(B) James Worthy

(C) Jimmy Black

(D) Phil Ford

165. Under Don Haskins in 1966, Texas Western College upset Kentucky to become the first NCAA men's basketball champion with an all-black starting lineup. What school did Texas Western become?

(A) Texas Christian

(B) Texas-El Paso

(C) Texas A&M

(D) Texas State

Answers from previous page:

163. D. The Bruins won 10 national titles under Wooden between 1963 and '75.

164. A. Jordan, just a freshman at the time, launched a long career of clutch shooting and winning championships when his 17-footer led the Tar Heels to victory.

165. B. In 1967, Texas Western College became known as the University of Texas at El Paso.

166. True or False: Cagney & Lacey was cancelled after the second season, but given new life thanks to the efforts of the fans.

167. In the heartwarming 1988 comedy Big, a 12-year-old boy's wish to be "big" comes true. Who directed the film?

(A) Garry Marshall

(B) Nora Ephron

(C) Penny Marshall

(D) Jon Turteltaub

168. True or False: Sharon Gless eventually married her Cagney & Lacey co-star, Martin Kove.

169. What year did the action adventure series The A-Team premiere?

(A) 1983

(B) 1984

(C) 1985

(D) 1986

166. True: The show was cancelled due to low ratings, but scores of fans wrote to the network expressing their unhappiness with the decision. The inundation of letters, coupled with a rise in ratings during summer reruns, changed the network's mind and the show was saved.

167. C. With Big, Penny Marshall became first female director to direct a movie that grossed more than $100 million at the box office.

168. False: In 1991, Gless married series executive producer Barney Rosenzweig. During the filming of the show, Rosenzweig was married to Cagney & Lacey creator Barbara Corday.

169. A. The show's first episode aired after Super Bowl XVII on January 30, 1983. It ran for a total of five seasons.

170. Where was the famous "giant piano" scene in Big filmed?

(A) On a Hollywood sound stage

(B) At Toys R Us

(C) In a New York warehouse

(D) At FAO Schwarz

171. True or False: Coincidentally, Cagney & Lacey happened to be filmed in building on Cagney Avenue.

172. The famous A-Team theme song was composed by Pete Carpenter, and which other popular television show composer?

(A) Jan Hammer

(B) Bill Conti

(C) Mike Post

(D) Jerrold Immel

173. What year did the sitcom Benson premiere?

(A) 1979

(B) 1980

(C) 1981

(D) 1982

170. D. The famous scene was filmed at the now-closed FAO Schwarz flagship store on Fifth Avenue. Robert Loggia has said that doubles were on hand to play the giant piano in case he and Tom Hanks weren't able to do it. This made them even more determined to perform the song themselves.

171. False: While the series was not filmed on "Cagney Avenue," it was, coincidentally, filmed in a studio on Lacy Street in Los Angeles!

172. C. The Emmy-winning Post has composed music for shows like The Greatest American Hero, Riptide, Quantum Leap, and Law & Order.

173. A. The series debuted in the fall of 1979 and ran for seven seasons.

174. Which professional football player appeared in a fifth-season episode of The A-Team as T.J. Bryant?

(A) Walter Payton

(B) Joe Namath

(C) Dan Marino

(D) Lawrence Taylor

175. Cheers remains one of the longest-running sitcoms in television history. How many seasons did it run?

(A) 9

(B) 10

(C) 11

(D) 12

176. True or False: The house used for exterior shots of the governor's mansion on Benson is the same house that was used years later for exterior shots of the Banks' residence on The Fresh Prince of Bel-Air.

174. B. The episode also featured former players Alan Autry, Jim Brown, and John Matuszak, who played the role of Sloth in the classic adventure comedy, The Goonies.

175. D. The show ran for 11 seasons, airing from 1982 until 1993.

176. False: Although the houses look quite similar, they are not the same house. The house used for Benson is located at 1365 S. Oakland Avenue in Pasadena, California, while the house used for The Fresh Prince of Bel-Air is located at 251 N. Bristol Avenue in Los Angeles. Both homes are reportedly good for maxin' and relaxin'.

177. Which future sitcom leading man made his acting debut on Benson?

(A) Steve Carrell

(B) Kelsey Grammer

(C) Jerry Seinfeld

(D) Bob Saget

178. Who was the first player to win the Heisman Trophy twice?

(A) Bo Jackson

(B) Archie Griffin

(C) Charles White

(D) Tim Brown

179. Which running back was the first player to rush for 20 touchdowns in a single season?

(A) John Riggins

(B) Emmitt Smith

(C) Chuck Muncie

(D) Joe Morris

177. C. Seinfeld appeared in two episodes as a delivery man and aspiring comic named Frankie.

178. B. Griffin, the Ohio State running back, won the award in 1974 and '75.

179. A. Riggins, still bruising at 34 years old, ran for 24 touchdowns for the Washington Redskins in 1983.

180. With "Terrible Towels" waving all around him, who was the first quarterback to win four Super Bowl championships?

181. True or **False:** Cheers used a laugh track instead of filming with a live audience.

182. Benson was considered a spin-off of which late '70s sitcom?

(A) Soap

(B) All in the Family

(C) Welcome Back, Kotter

(D) The Jeffersons

183. Which now-famous actor guest starred on four seasons of Dallas when he was still an unknown?

(A) Tom Hanks

(B) Matt Damon

(C) George Clooney

(D) Brad Pitt

180. Terry Bradshaw led the Pittsburgh Steelers to four Super Bowl wins during a six-year stretch beginning with the 1974 NFL season.

181. False – Although the show was filmed in front of an audience and the laughter was genuine, viewers often complained about the "loud laugh track." In the second season, the familiar, "Cheers was filmed before a live studio audience" was added before each episode as a disclaimer, but some viewers continued to complain about the nonexistent "laugh track"!

182. A. Benson proved to be the more popular of the two shows, lasting an impressive seven seasons, while Soap ran for four.

183. D. Pitt appeared in four episodes in the eleventh season. He played Randy, the boyfriend of Charlie Wade (played by actress Shalane McCall).

184. Which actor plays John "Hannibal" Smith in The A-Team?

(A) Larry Hagman

(B) Harry Dean Stanton

(C) Perry King

(D) George Peppard

185. Rene Auberjonois, who plays Clayton Runnymede Endicott III in Benson, would later appear in which out-of-this-world series?

(A) The X-Files

(B) Star Trek: The Next Generation

(C) Battlestar Galactica

(D) Star Trek: Deep Space Nine

186. Who plays psychiatrist and regular Cheers patron Frasier Crane?

(A) Bill Paxton

(B) Peter Gallagher

(C) Kelsey Grammer

(D) David Hyde Pierce

184. **D.** Peppard was already an accomplished actor before joining The A-Team, famously playing Paul Varjak opposite Audrey Hepburn's Holly Golightly in Breakfast at Tiffany's. He also appeared in How the West Was Won, The Carpetbaggers, and The Blue Max.

185. **D.** Auberjonois spent seven seasons playing the alien Odo on Star Trek: Deep Space Nine. He continues to appear in TV roles. And he wasn't the only future alien on the show: his co-star on Benson, Ethan Phillips, who played press secretary Pete Downey, would later star as Neelix in Star Trek: Voyager.

186. **C.** Frasier was intended to be a temporary, seven-episode character, but was so popular he was made a regular. Grammer went on to play the same character in Frasier, portraying the same character for a total of 20 years. This was a record for an American actor in a comedy series.

187. Who shot J.R.?

(A) Lucy Ewing

(B) Cliff Barnes

(C) Clayton Farlow

(D) Kristin Shepard

188. How many viewers tuned in for the finale of M*A*S*H in 1983?

(A) 101 million

(B) 131 million

(C) 121 million

(D) 111 million

189. Mr. T is probably best-known for his role on The A-Team as B.A. Baracus. What is his character's first name?

(A) Barry

(B) Bert

(C) Bosco

(D) Benedict

187. D. Kristin was J.R.'s sister-in-law and jilted ex-lover. But there were scores of characters who might've had reasons to shoot J.R., and the writers wanted to keep their options open. So several characters, including Lucy Ewing and Jock Ewing, were filmed firing the gun before it was decided that Kristin was the culprit. The Simpsons played on this idea in a similar cliffhanger: Who Shot Mr. Burns?

188. D. The finale, in which Hawkeye slowly unravels a terrible and moving psychological trauma with the help of the series's long-running psychiatrist, broke the record set in 1980 by the conclusion of "Who Shot J.R.?" on Dallas.

189. C. Incidentally, the "B.A." in Bosco Baracus's name is said to stand for "Bad Attitude."

190. The creator of Benson, Susan Harris, also created which other popular sitcom?

(A) The Facts of Life

(B) Cheers

(C) The Golden Girls

(D) Family Ties

191. What was the CIA research project MKULTRA?

192. True or False: Benson was the first network series to show characters using the internet.

193. Which actor plays The A-Team's "Howling Mad" Murdock?

(A) Dwight Schultz

(B) Stephen Collins

(C) Robert Hays

(D) Jameson Parker

190. C. Harris was nominated for six Emmys for her work on The Golden Girls, and won in 1987 for Outstanding Comedy Series.

191. From the mid-1950s through at least the early 1970s, thousands of unwitting Americans and Canadians became part of a bizarre CIA research project codenamed MKULTRA. Participants were secretly "brainwashed"—drugged with LSD and other hallucinogens, subjected to electro-convulsive shock therapy, and manipulated with abusive mind-control techniques.

192. True: In an episode where the staff runs nuclear war simulations, the computer network they use is called "ARPANET." This network was used by the U.S. government and was a precursor to today's internet.

193. A. Schultz had a small but memorable role as Lt. Reginald Barclay on Star Trek: The Next Generation and Star Trek: Voyager. More recently, he's lent his voice to dozens of animated shows and video games.

194. Cheers waitress Carla (played by Rhea Perlman) has quite the complicated full name. How many different names does she have in total?

(A) Six

(B) Seven

(C) Eight

(D) Nine

195. Which of these college football greats did not win the Heisman Trophy?

(A) Bo Jackson

(B) Herschel Walker

(C) Joe Theismann

(D) Billy Sims

196. Who composed the well-known theme song for Dallas?

(A) Lance Rubin

(B) John Scott

(C) Ken Harrison

(D) Jerrold Immel

Answers from previous page:

194. D. Carla's full name is Carla Maria Victoria Angelina Teresa Apollonia Lozupone Tortelli LeBec. Whew!

195. C. Though he changed the pronunciation of his name to rhyme with the fabled award while quarterbacking Notre Dame, Theismann was runner-up to Jim Plunkett in the 1970 Heisman voting.

196. D. Immel also wrote music for Gunsmoke, Knot's Landing, and Walker, Texas Ranger.

197. Name the first team to win five Super Bowl championships.

198. True or False: Even though Cheers took place in a bar, no one was ever seen leaving drunk to drive home.

199. Which actor plays Benson?

(A) George Harris

(B) Ben Vereen

(C) Sherman Hemsley

(D) Robert Guillaume

200. Which of the following college football stars went on to play professional basketball?

(A) Charlie Ward

(B) Deion Sanders

(C) Joe Montana

(D) Bo Jackson

197. The San Francisco 49ers were the "Team of the 1980s" with four Super Bowl titles that decade, and they added a fifth after the 1994 season. The following year, the Dallas Cowboys won their fifth.

198. True – The writers wanted their characters to set a responsible example to the audience, and the show was recognized by anti-drinking and driving groups for helping to promote designated driver programs.

199. D. While Benson is undoubtedly Guillaume's most famous character, he had a prolific career with dozens of appearances in television, film, and theater. The Tony-nominated actor had a popular run playing the Phantom on Broadway in The Phantom of the Opera, has guest-starred on Diagnosis Murder, 8 Simple Rules, and CSI: Crime Scene Investigation, and was memorable as the voice of Rafiki in The Lion King.

200. A. While Sanders and Jackson played pro baseball, it was Florida State's Ward who starred on the hardwood for the New York Knicks.

201. Who was the quarterback for Stanford when Cal beat the Cardinal on "The Play," considered the most amazing finish to any college football game in history, in 1982?

(A) Jim Plunkett

(B) Turk Schonert

(C) John Elway

(D) Steve Stenstrom

202. When Barbara Bel Geddes took time off during the seventh and eighth seasons of Dallas for health reasons, what star of '50s and '60s television took her place as Miss Ellie?

(A) Barbara Billingsley

(B) Harriet Nelson

(C) Jane Wyatt

(D) Donna Reed

203. Which character from Cheers never appeared on the spin-off, Frasier?

(A) Rebecca

(B) Sam

(C) Woody

(D) Diane

201. C. Elway had driven Stanford to a 20-19 lead in the final minute before Cal returned the ensuing kickoff for the winning touchdown, thanks to the most exciting series of laterals in football history.

202. D. Reed is known not only for her popular television series The Donna Reed Show, but also for starring in one of the most beloved Christmas movies of all time, It's a Wonderful Life.

203. A. Kirstie Alley refused to appear on Frasier, as its focus on psychiatry conflicted with her Scientology beliefs.

204. True or False: All ten of the actors who appeared as regulars on Cheers were nominated for Emmy Awards.

205. How many seasons did the drama Dallas air on television?

(A) 12

(B) 13

(C) 14

(D) 15

206. Who was the only cast member of Dallas to ever win an Emmy for the show?

(A) Barbara Bel Geddes

(B) Larry Hagman

(C) Jim Davis

(D) Linda Gray

207. True or False: The only reason J.R. Ewing was alive after Dallas's season three cliffhanger was because Larry Hagman's contract demands were met.

204. True – Ted Danson, George Wendt, John Ratzenberger, Kirstie Alley, Shelley Long, Rhea Perlman, Kelsey Grammer, Woody Harrelson, Nicholas Colasanto and Bebe Neuwirth were all nominated during the course of the show's run. Danson, Alley, Long, Perlman, Harrelson, and Neuwirth all won awards.

205. C. The popular soap-opera style show spanned the entire '80s decade, running from 1978 until 1991.

206. A. Bel Geddes was nominated three times, and won once. Larry Hagman, Jim Davis, and Linda Gray were also nominated, but never won.

207. True: Hagman was renegotiating his contract at the end of season three, and the cliffhanger gave the producers the opportunity to either let J.R. live (if his contract demands were met) or let the character die (if his demands were too outlandish). Hagman got the raise he wanted, and J.R. lived to see another season! Savvy viewers now understand that dramatic end-of-season events often cover for similar negotiations.

208. Which Friends alum played Lauren, Alex's girlfriend, for the last two seasons of Family Ties?

(A) Lisa Kudrow

(B) Courteney Cox

(C) Jennifer Aniston

(D) Maggie Wheeler

209. Early in his career, Tiger Woods set Jack Nicklaus' PGA record for major championship victories as one of his foremost goals. How many majors did Nicklaus win?

(A) 12

(B) 15

(C) 18

(D) 21

210. For seven straight seasons between 1969 and '75, a Boston Bruin led the NHL in scoring. Five of those times, it was Phil Esposito. Which Hall of Fame defenseman accounted for the other two?

208. B. A then-unknown Cox appeared in the final two seasons of the show. Although there were rumors that she and Fox were dating, both denied the stories.

209. C. Nicklaus won 18 majors, beginning with a U.S. Open title as a 22-year-old and ending with a stunning Masters win at age 46 in 1986.

210. Bobby Orr. Despite his role as a "blue liner," the sensational Orr led the NHL in total points in 1969-70 and '74-75.

211. Which Hall of Famer, two years after retiring, returned to the ice in his mid-40s to suit up for the WHA's Houston Aeros with his sons, Mark and Marty, and wound up winning the WHA scoring title?

212. True or False: Dynasty was surprisingly popular in the former Yugoslavia.

213. True or False: Arthur Ashe was the first African-American to win Wimbledon.

214. Name the American diver who became the first man in Olympic history to sweep both the 3-meter springboard and 10-meter platform gold medals in back-to-back Games.

(A) Bob Webster

(B) Gary Tobian

(C) Greg Louganis

(D) David Boudia

211. Gordie Howe. Howe wound up playing six WHA seasons, and later returned to the NHL at age 51 as Mark's teammate with the Hartford Whalers in 1979-80.

212. True: The show was extremely popular in the southeastern European country. Incidentally, Catherine Oxenberg, who played Amanda Bedford Carrington in 53 episodes, was the daughter of Princess Elizabeth of Yugoslavia. Perhaps this explains the country's admiration for the show!

213. False. While Ashe was the first African-American man to win Wimbledon, and was also the first to attain the world's No. 1 ranking, it was Althea Gibson's Wimbledon victory back in 1957 that broke the color barrier at the All England Lawn Tennis and Croquet Club.

214. C. Louganis, considered the greatest American diver of all time, won gold in both events in 1984 and '88.

215. True or False: Composer Jerrold Immel, who wrote the theme for Dallas, also wrote the theme for Dynasty.

216. How many seasons did the drama Hill Street Blues air?

(A) Five

(B) Six

(C) Seven

(D) Eight

217. True or False: Wayne Gretzky is the all-time NHL leader in goals, assists and points.

218. Who sings the famous theme song "Footloose"?

(A) Christopher Cross

(B) Hall & Oates

(C) Kenny Loggins

(D) Kenny Rogers

215. False: The Dynasty theme was written by Oscar-winner Bill Conti, who also wrote the themes for Cagney & Lacey, Falcon Crest, and the Dynasty spin-off, The Colbys.

216. C. The show ran from January 1981 until May 1987.

217. True, and it's not even close. "The Great One" totaled 894 goals and 1,963 assists for 2,857 points.

218. C. The film opens with a shot of dozens of dancing feet, set to the upbeat song. The feet with the gold shoes actually belong to Loggins himself.

219. True or False: The weekly wardrobe budget for Dynasty was $20,000.

220. What are the three "statistics" comprise a "Gordie Howe hat trick"?

221. Why were the 1972 Munich Olympic Games suspended for about 34 hours?

222. Jean Smart left Designing Women after the fifth season, and Charlene was replaced by sister Carlene. Who played the part?

(A) Jan Hooks

(B) Julia Duffy

(C) Patricia Richardson

(D) Catherine Hicks

219. False: The budget was a whopping $35,000 per week! Costume designer Nolan Miller designed approximately 3,000 costumes over the duration of the series. The name Dynasty still stands in for a certain kind of shoulder-padded and dramatic '80s "high fashion."

220. A goal, an assist and a fight in the same game comprise a "Gordie Howe hat trick," a nod to the kind of effort that was not unfamiliar to the longtime Detroit Red Wings great.

221. Because of a hostage crisis. Palestinian terrorists broke into the Israeli quarters, killed two Israeli athletes and took nine hostages. Those hostages were later killed in a failed rescue attempt.

222. A. Hicks spent five seasons on Saturday Night Live in the late '80s, where her many impersonations included Hillary Clinton, Kathie Lee Gifford, Nancy Reagan, and Diane Sawyer.

223. Who, in 1975-76, became the first Montreal Canadiens player to win the NHL scoring title since Bernie "Boom Boom" Geoffrion 15 years earlier?

(A) Steve Shutt

(B) Guy LaFleur

(C) Yvan Cournoyer

(D) Bob Gainey

224. The Keaton family in Family Ties consists of Steven, Elyse, Mallory, Jennifer, and, of course, Alex P. Keaton, played by which actor?

(A) Ralph Macchio

(B) Michael J. Fox

(C) Patrick Dempsey

(D) John Cusack

225. Which of the following players won the most Grand Slam singles titles?

(A) Bjorn Borg

(B) John McEnroe

(C) Jimmy Connors

(D) Ivan Lendl

223. B. LaFleur began a string of three consecutive years as the NHL's top point-getter.

224. B. Fox almost didn't get the part. Producers thought the 5'4" Fox was too short to believably play the son of Meredith Baxter Birney and Michael Gross, who are 5'7" and 6'4", respectively.

225. A. Borg won 11 Grand Slam titles—the French Open six times and Wimbledon five. Lendl and Connors totaled eight titles apiece, while McEnroe collected seven.

226. Which future Oscar-winner guest appeared on Golden Girls as a police officer investigating jewel thieves?

(A) Marisa Tomei

(B) George Clooney

(C) Brad Pitt

(D) Julianne Moore

227. Name the American professional soccer team that incomparable Brazilian star Pele came out of retirement to play for in 1975.

228. Which Grand Ole Opry singer performs the Growing Pains theme song, "As Long As We've Got Each Other"?

(A) Charlie Pride

(B) Larry Gatlin

(C) Bill Monroe

(D) B.J. Thomas

229. True or False: Ronald Reagan once stated that Family Ties was his favorite show of the 80s.

226. B. Clooney appeared on an episode in 1987, years before his breakout role as Dr. Doug Ross on ER.

227. The New York Cosmos.

228. D. Thomas is perhaps best known for performing the songs "Raindrops Keep Fallin' on My Head" and "Hooked on a Feeling." In later seasons, the theme was sung as a duet between Thomas and Jennifer Warnes.

229. True – It certainly couldn't have hurt that Alex P. Keaton was a staunch Republican. Reportedly, Reagan even offered to appear in an episode – too bad that didn't pan out!

230. Name the sprinter who, with six medals in the 1980s and '90s, became the most decorated woman in U.S. track and field history.

(A) Gail Devers

(B) Marion Jones

(C) Florence Griffith-Joyner

(D) Jackie Joyner-Kersee

231. Who was the first cast member to be nominated for an Emmy Award for their work on the show Designing Women?

(A) Delta Burke

(B) Dixie Carter

(C) Meshach Taylor

(D) Alice Ghostley

232. After more than 60 years, tennis was reinstated as an Olympic medal sport for the 1988 Games in Seoul. Who won the women's singles title that year?

(A) Jennifer Capriati

(B) Steffi Graf

(C) Martina Navratilova

(D) Pam Shriver

230. D. Joyner-Kersee has been referred to as the "First Lady of American track and field."

231. C. In total, the show received 18 Emmy nominations, but only three members of the cast were ever nominated. Taylor was first, followed by Burke and Ghostley. The show only won a single Emmy, for "Outstanding Achievement in Hairstyling."

232. B. Graf, then representing West Germany, defeated Gabriela Sabatini in the final.

233. How many seasons did the comedy The Facts of Life air?

(A) 6

(B) 7

(C) 8

(D) 9

234. At which school does the movie Real Genius take place?

(A) Los Angeles Tech

(B) Southern California University

(C) Pacific Tech

(D) California College

235. Kevin Bacon plays the part of Ren MacCormack in the original 1984 version of Footloose. Which city does Ren live in before moving to the small-town Midwest?

(A) New York

(B) Los Angeles

(C) Chicago

(D) Dallas

233. D. The Facts of Life premiered in 1979 and ran until 1988.

234. C. In the movie, the school is called Pacific Tech, and it was filmed at Pomona College and Occidental College. But the story was very loosely based on actual events which occurred at the California Institute of Technology in Pasadena, California.

235. C. John Travolta, well known at the time for his dancing moves in movies like Saturday Night Fever and Grease, was offered the part of the Chicago boy who moves to a small town, but he turned it down. Ren became an iconic role for Keven Bacon.

236. Who created Hill Street Blues?

(A) Steven Bochco

(B) David E. Kelley

(C) Dick Wolf

(D) Stephen J. Cannell

237. Muhammad Ali and Joe Frazier battled in three of the greatest heavyweight bouts of all time. What was the nickname given to their classic third bout, won by Ali when Frazier could not answer the bell for the 15th round?

(A) Thrilla in Manila

(B) Rumble in the Jungle

(C) Slugfest in Somalia

(D) The Showdown

238. How many seasons did the comedy The Golden Girls run?

(A) 6

(B) 7

(C) 8

(D) 9

236. A. Bochco is known for producing and writing crime dramas, including L.A. Law, NYPD Blue, and Murder in the First.

237. A. Manila was the site of the best fight in the trilogy. After his victory, Ali called the pounding he took "the closest thing to dying that I know of."

238. B. The show ran from 1985 until 1992, and a short-lived spin off called The Golden Palace aired from 1992 to 1993.

239. On Designing Women, which actress plays Mary Jo's best friend, Charlene Frazier?

(A) Delta Burke

(B) Annie Potts

(C) Karen Allen

(D) Jean Smart

240. True or False: The Canada Cup hockey series began as a tournament pitting the best players from Canada against the best from the United States.

241. True or False: Alex P. Keaton eventually fulfilled his political dreams and became a senator in Ohio.

242. True or False: Matthew Broderick was the first choice for the role of Alex P. Keaton.

Answers from previous page:

239. D. Smart has been married to actor Richard Gilliland since 1987. The two met on the set of Designing Women, when Gilliland guest starred as Mary Jo's boyfriend, J.D. Shackleford.

340. False. The tournament got its origin in 1972 as a series between the best from Canada and the top players from the Soviet Union. It was later renamed the World Cup of Hockey and expanded to include other countries.

241. True – Michael J. Fox went on to star as Michael Flaherty in Spin City. In one episode, we find out that Flaherty becomes an environmental activist in Washington D.C., where he crosses paths with none other than Ohio Senator Alex P. Keaton!

242. True – Broderick was offered the role for the sitcom, which filmed in Los Angeles, but instead he chose to remain in New York City to be near his gravely ill father.

243. Which Saved by the Bell star appeared on Golden Girls as one of Dorothy's pupils?

(A) Elizabeth Berkley

(B) Mario Lopez

(C) Lark Voorhies

(D) Mark-Paul Gosselaar

244. After suffering his first loss as a collegian during the championship match of his final NCAA tournament, which wrestling legend cruised to a gold medal in the 1972 Olympics without surrendering a single point in any match?

(A) Rulon Gardner

(B) Bruce Baumgartner

(C) Tom Brands

(D) Dan Gable

245. Which popular 80s actress was a member of the original cast in the first season of The Facts of Life?

(A) Molly Ringwald

(B) Ally Sheedy

(C) Lea Thompson

(D) Elisabeth Shue

243. B. Lopez guest starred as a boy who writes a prize-winning essay about America. But Dorothy later discovers that her favorite student is in the country illegally. Wow, this plot has not aged well!

244. D. Gable, who enjoyed unprecedented success as both an athlete and college coach, made one of the most amazing runs in Olympic history by shutting out each of his 1972 Olympic opponents.

245. A. In the first season, there were seven main girls in the cast, but the producers decided to retool the show for the second season. They pared down the cast to four girls, and Ringwald didn't make the cut.

246. Which of the following greats is not a member of the Montreal Canadiens' Ring of Honor?

(A) Ken Dryden

(B) Larry Robinson

(C) Maurice Richard

(D) Stan Mikita

247. Who was the first man to accumulate $1 million in career earnings as a professional bowler?

(A) Earl Anthony

(B) Walter Ray Williams Jr.

(C) Pete Weber

(D) Mark Roth

248. In what year did Designing Women premiere?

(A) 1984

(B) 1985

(C) 1986

(D) 1987

Answers from previous page:

246. D. While the others powered the Montreal Canadiens to dynasty status, Mikita was a Chicago Blackhawks legend.

247. A. Anthony, a dominant force in the 1970s and '80s, finished with more than $1.4 million in career earnings and a record 41 titles on the regular PBA Tour.

248. C. Designing Women premiered in 1986 and ran for seven seasons.

249. Which fun-loving 1988 Olympic bobsled team inspired the 1993 film Cool Runnings?

(A) Canada

(B) Jamaica

(C) Norway

(D) France

250. Hill Street Blues was considered the first "ensemble drama" on television, with many different actors receiving equal screen and story time. Who played Captain Frank Furillo?

(A) Michael Warren

(B) James Sikking

(C) Charles Haid

(D) Daniel J. Travanti

251. Before the show was produced, what was the working title for Dynasty?

(A) Denver

(B) The Carringtons

(C) Oil

(D) Wealth

Answers from previous page:

249. B. The Jamaican bobsled team gained a cult following after qualifying for the Calgary Games.

250. D. Travanti has recently guest starred on notable television shows such as Grey's Anatomy, Criminal Minds, and NCIS: Los Angeles, and he played the part of Gerald "Babe" McGantry on the critically acclaimed Boss with Kelsey Grammer.

251. C. The show's creators, Richard and Esther Shapiro, tentatively titled their series Oil, but it was changed to Dynasty before it hit the television airwaves. Instead, the first episode of the series was titled Oil.

252. What's the last name of the American brother duo from St. Louis that brought home two Olympic boxing gold medals from the Montreal Games in 1976?

253. True or False: Director Quentin Tarantino appeared on The Golden Girls before finding success as a director.

254. True or False: Queen Elizabeth was a huge fan of The Golden Girls.

255. In what sport are Laird Hamilton, Kelly Slater, and Duke Kahanamoku considered to rank among the greatest athletes of all time?

252. Spinks. Leon won the light heavyweight division gold medal while Michael ruled the middleweight class. Sugar Ray Leonard also won gold for the U.S. that year. Other famous U.S. boxing gold medalists have included George Foreman (1968), Joe Frazier (1964) and Muhammad Ali (1960, as Cassius Clay).

253. True: Tarantino played an Elvis impersonator at Sophia's wedding in a fourth-season episode.

254. True: The Queen Mum was such a fan of the show that she invited the cast to perform for her live at 1988's Royal Variety Performance in London.

255. Surfing.

256. Who plays the patriarch of the Growing Pains family, Jason Seaver?

(A) Alan Thicke

(B) Michael Gross

(C) Ted Danson

(D) Ted Wass

257. Which star was the youngest cast member on Golden Girls?

(A) Rue McClanahan

(B) Betty White

(C) Estelle Getty

(D) Bea Arthur

258. Which actress plays fiery feminist Julia Sugarbaker in Designing Women?

(A) Lily Tomlin

(B) Delta Burke

(C) Annie Potts

(D) Dixie Carter

Answers from previous page:

256. A. Although he was best known for his role on Growing Pains, Thicke had quite a prolific and diverse career. He authored books, hosted game shows and reality shows, and composed the theme songs for Diff'rent Strokes and The Facts of Life. Sadly, the beloved TV dad passed away in late 2016.

257. A. Rue McClanahan was about a decade younger than the other cast members. Betty White was the oldest.

258. D. Carter got her start in theater in New York City, and then branched out to television after moving to California. Some of her credits include Diff'rent Strokes, Family Law, and Desperate Housewives.

259. Name the school that broke Oklahoma State's record by winning nine consecutive NCAA Division I wrestling team championships from 1978 to '86.

(A) Iowa

(B) Iowa State

(C) Minnesota

(D) Penn State

260. Dynasty aired on ABC, and was considered a competitor to what show on CBS?

(A) Dallas

(B) Knots Landing

(C) Falcon Crest

(D) Hart to Hart

261. What does the "P" in Alex P. Keaton stand for?

(A) Philip

(B) Paul

(C) Patrick

(D) Nothing

259. B. The Dan Gable-coached Hawkeyes surpassed Oklahoma State, which had won seven in a row in the 1930s and '40s.

260. A. Dynasty was often considered a "more glamorous" version of Dallas, with both shows depicting wealthy oil tycoons and their dysfunctional families.

261. D. We never find out what Alex's middle initial stands for. Incidentally, the "J" in Michael J. Fox's name is also a made-up initial – he chose it when he registered his name with the Screen Actor's Guild. His real middle name is Andrew.

262. Which hard-shooting Chicago Blackhawks legend, nicknamed the "Golden Jet," also gave the NHL the "Golden Brett" in the form of his superstar son?

263. How do most episodes of Hill Street Blues begin?

(A) A car chase

(B) A roll call

(C) A city skyline view

(D) A 911 call

264. Name the American track and field superstar who won four consecutive Olympic long jump gold medals from 1984 to '96.

265. Which of the following teams did not join the NHL in the 1990s?

(A) Winnipeg Jets

(B) Tampa Bay Lightning

(C) Ottawa Senators

(D) San Jose Sharks

262. Bobby Hull. Hull scored 610 NHL goals. His son, Brett, tallied 741.

263. B. Throughout the series, five different characters started each episode with roll call: Sgt. Phil Esterhaus (played by Michael Conrad), whose line "let's be careful out there" became a television catchprase; Lt. Henry Goldblume (Joe Spano); Sgt. Lucy Bates (Betty Thomas); Sgt. Stan Jablonski (Robert Prosky); and Lt. Howard Hunter (James Sikking).

264. Carl Lewis. Lewis matched his hero, Jesse Owens, with four gold medals in the 1984 Games. One of those was in the long jump, which he went on to win at the next three Olympics as well.

265. A. The Winnipeg Jets joined the NHL from the WHA in the 1970s and played until '96, then came back to life in 2012-13 when the Atlanta Thrashers moved north.

266. Who was the creator of the popular sitcom Designing Women?

(A) Sherry Coben

(B) Linda Bloodworth-Thomason

(C) Agnes Nixon

(D) Susan Harris

267. What was the nickname of Eddie Edwards, the British plasterer-turned-ski jumper whose inept performance in the 1988 Calgary Games prompted a rule making it more difficult for marginal athletes to qualify for the Olympics?

(A) Ace

(B) Rocket Man

(C) The Eagle

(D) E-Dawg

268. On The Facts of Life, what is the name of Blair's cousin who makes several appearances on the show? And as a bonus, what was the character's landmark achievement?

(A) Jenny

(B) Geri

(C) Georgia

(D) Jessica

266. B. Bloodworth-Thomason was also the creator of another popular CBS show, Evening Shade. In addition to creating Designing Women, she also wrote many of the episodes.

267. C. Eddie "The Eagle" became popular with fans for his last-place finish in 70-meter ski jumping and his next-to-last showing in the 90-meter, where he finished ahead of a French jumper who broke his leg.

268. B. Geri, played by actress Geri Jewell, was the first featured television character to have a physical disability. Jewell, who was born with cerebral palsy, is now an author, radio personality, and motivational speaker.

269. Which political figure guest starred on an episode of Dynasty?

(A) Gerald Ford

(B) Henry Kissinger

(C) Betty Ford

(D) All of the above

270. During the 2012 Games, American swimmer Michael Phelps raised his total to 22 medals (18 gold) to become the most decorated Olympian of all time. Who held the previous mark for most medals, regardless of sport?

(A) Mark Spitz

(B) Carl Lewis

(C) Larisa Latynina

(D) Nadia Comaneci

271. What is the title of the famous theme song for the show Golden Girls?

(A) You've Got a Friend

(B) We'll Always Be Friends

(C) Thank You for Being a Friend

(D) Friendship Never Ends

269. D. Former President Gerald Ford, his wife Betty, and former Secretary of State Henry Kissinger all guest starred as themselves in the season-four episode, Carousel.

270. C. Latynina, a Soviet-era gymnast, accumulated 18 Olympic medals. Phelps's accomplishment caused a lot of discussion about the number of separate but similar swimming events.

271. C. The song was written and originally recorded by singer Andrew Gold in 1978. It was re-recorded by Cynthia Fee for the show.

272. True or False: Footloose was loosely based on real events.

273. Where is the show Dynasty set?

(A) Houston, Texas

(B) Los Angeles, California

(C) Atlanta, Georgia

(D) Denver, Colorado

274. Who was the highest-scoring defenseman in NHL history?

(A) Bobby Orr

(B) Ray Bourque

(C) Denis Potvin

(D) Al Macinnis

272. True: The story was inspired by events in the small farming town of Elmore City, Oklahoma. Dancing had been banned in the town since its founding in 1861, but in 1978 a group of high schoolers was able to get the ban overturned and they won the right to dance at their prom.

273. D. Although the show was set in Denver, the home used as the exterior of the 48-room Carrington mansion was filmed at the Filoli estate in Woodside, California. The home is on the National Register of Historic Places and is open to the public.

274. B. Ray Bourque set NHL records for defensemen with 410 goals, 1,169 assists and 1,579 points between 1979 and 2001.

275. Which Stand By Me star did NOT have a cameo on the show Family Ties?

(A) Jerry O'Connell

(B) River Phoenix

(C) Wil Wheaton

(D) Corey Feldman

276. In Designing Women, who plays divorced single mom Mary Jo Shively?

(A) Dana Delany

(B) Annie Potts

(C) Delta Burke

(D) Dixie Carter

277. What famous "goon" holds the NHL career record with 3,966 penalty minutes?

(A) Tie Domi

(B) Tiger Williams

(C) Marty McSorley

(D) Dale Hunter

275. A. River Phoenix, Wil Wheaton, and Corey Feldman all made appearances on the show as friends and classmates of Jennifer Keaton.

276. B. Potts has been busy since her stint on Designing Women, appearing in shows like Any Day Now, Joan of Arcadia, The Fosters, and Chicago Med. And she had a memorable role as Janine Melnitz, the cynical assistant, in the Ghostbusters franchise.

277. B. While the others were all renowned scrappers in their own right, no one served more penalty time than Dave "Tiger" Williams, who prowled the ice from 1974 to '88.

278. Which big star almost played the part of Jason Seaver on Growing Pains?

(A) Kevin Costner

(B) Bruce Willis

(C) Sam Neill

(D) Kevin Kline

279. In what year did the United States win its first gold medal in Olympic ice hockey?

(A) 1960

(B) 1968

(C) 1972

(D) 1980

280. If the famous kitchen in The Golden Girls' house looks familiar, that may be because the set was first used for which short-lived early '80s sitcom?

(A) It Takes Two

(B) Life with Lucy

(C) Three's a Crowd

(D) Amanda's

278. B. Willis was up for the part of Jason Seaver, but instead was cast in the show Moonlighting, which debuted the same year as Growing Pains.

279. A. Twenty years before the "Miracle on Ice," Team USA won all seven games to win its first gold on home ice in Squaw Valley, CA in 1960.

280. A. It Takes Two aired for just one season and starred Richard Crenna, Patty Duke, a very young Helen Hunt, and Anthony Edwards with a full head of hair!

281. True or False: Los Angeles has hosted the Olympic Summer Games twice.

282. Name the announcer whose famous line— "Do you believe in miracles? Yes!"—helped define the 1980 American hockey victory in Lake Placid as the "Miracle on Ice."

283. Name the American speed skater who, in 1980, became the first athlete in any Olympics—summer or winter—to win five gold medals in one Games.

281. True. L.A. hosted the Games in 1932 and 1984.

282. Al Michaels. Michaels broadcast the line in the final seconds of Team USA's medal-round victory over the heavily-favored Soviet Union. The Americans then beat Finland to wrap up the gold.

283. Eric Heiden. The 21-year-old from Wisconsin set Olympic records in all five events, including a world record in the 10,000 meters.

284. Which coach tops the NHL career victory list?

(A) Scotty Bowman

(B) Mike Keenan

(C) Al Arbour

(D) Dick Irvin

285. What year did the drama Dynasty premiere?

(A) 1980

(B) 1981

(C) 1982

(D) 1983

286. True or False: To this day, Kevin Bacon loves to hear the song "Footloose," and often breaks out dancing when he hears it.

284. A. Bowman, with 1,244 career victories, is the only coach in NHL history with more than 1,000.

285. B. The series debuted in January 1981, and ran for nine seasons, until 1989.

286. False: Bacon has actually gone so far as to tip DJs NOT to play the song. He says that even though he performed some of the dancing moves himself, much of his dancing in the film was performed by Peter Tramm, his dance double.

287. Which of the following U.S. swimming greats won the fewest Olympic medals?

(A) Dara Torres

(B) Natalie Coughlin

(C) Jenny Thompson

(D) Mark Spitz

288. Hill Street Blues won a record-breaking eight Emmy awards in its first season, a feat later matched by NYPD Blue and ER. Which show finally broke the record?

(A) Law & Order

(B) Ally McBeal

(C) The West Wing

(D) 24

289. Which of the following teams was not one of the NHL's "Original Six" franchises?

(A) Boston Bruins

(B) Chicago Blackhawks

(C) Montreal Canadiens

(D) Philadelphia Flyers

287. D. Though he set a record (since broken by Michael Phelps) with seven gold medals in a single Olympics, Spitz falls below the women listed in career medals with 11. As of the 2012 London Games, Torres, Coughlin and Thompson had each passed him with 12.

288. C. The West Wing won nine Emmys in its first season.

289. D. The Philadelphia Flyers arrived in the NHL's 1967 expansion. In addition to Chicago, Montreal and Boston, the Original Six included the New York Rangers, Toronto Maple Leafs and Detroit Red Wings.

290. The Golden Girls include Sophia Petrillo, her daughter Dorothy Zbornak, and friends Rose Nylund and Blanche Devereaux. Where do they all live?

(A) Los Angeles

(B) Miami

(C) Ft. Lauderdale

(D) Savannah

291. What is Mr. Belvedere's full name?

(A) Leon Atticus

(B) Leroy Achilles

(C) Len Alastair

(D) Lynn Aloysius

292. True or False: Bob Newhart got the idea for the show Newhart after he himself spent time at a Vermont inn.

290. B. Although the girls all hail from different locations, they end up together in a house in Miami, complete with very Floridian wicker furniture.

291. D. Lynn Aloysius Belvedere was first introduced on-screen in the 1948 film Sitting Pretty, where he was played by Clifton Webb. Webb was nominated for a Best Actor Oscar for the role.

292. False: Newhart got the idea for the show after people-watching at a Hilton hotel in Seattle. He pitched his idea to Taxi writer Barry Kemp, who suggested the inn should be set in Vermont instead of Seattle. Newhart agreed, noting, "After you've done three or four rain jokes, you've kind of run out of material as far as Seattle is concerned."

293. The creator of Knight Rider, Glen A. Larson, was also the creator of which sci-fi show?

(A) Star Trek

(B) Stargate

(C) Battlestar Galactica

(D) Farscape

294. Who composed the chart-topping Miami Vice theme?

(A) Jan Hammer

(B) Harold Faltermeyer

(C) Mike Post

(D) Dana Kaproff

295. How many seasons did the dramedy Moonlighting air?

(A) Four

(B) Five

(C) Six

(D) Seven

293. C. Larson also created The Fall Guy, and co-created the shows B.J. and the Bear, Quincy M.E., and Magnum P.I.

294. A. Miami Vice Theme became the first television show theme song to hit #1 on the Billboard chart since Henry Mancini's theme for the show Peter Gunn in 1959.

295. B. The show debuted in 1985 and ran until 1989. Most episodes of hour-long shows have shooting schedules of about seven days, but Moonlighting episodes often took twice as long to shoot. Because of the delay, most seasons averaged only 15 episodes, instead of the 20-plus episodes most hour-long shows produce.

296. In what year did the action drama Knight Rider premiere?

(A) 1982

(B) 1983

(C) 1984

(D) 1985

297. True or False: Mr. Belvedere was only the second sitcom to feature a character with the AIDS virus.

298. Which legendary director had a cameo appearance on Moonlighting?

(A) Woody Allen

(B) Orson Welles

(C) Mel Brooks

(D) Sydney Pollack

296. **A. Knight Rider ran for four seasons, until 1986.**

297. **False: The show was actually the very first sitcom to talk openly about the disease. In one episode, Wesley finds out that his friend Danny has contracted HIV, and he must deal with the fear and prejudice surrounding the illness. Mr. Belvedere, of course, helps him to understand that he and his classmates can still be friends with the boy.**

298. **B. Welles introduced an episode titled "The Dream Sequence Always Rings Twice," which was mostly shot in black and white. Sadly, Welles passed away five days before the episode was broadcast, and a caption dedicated the episode to his memory.**

299. True or False: Henry Fonda and Katherine Hepburn appear in the opening credits of Newhart.

300. True or False: Bruce Willis was offered the part of John McClane in Die Hard right after Moonlighting ended.

301. True or False: Christopher Hewitt, who died in 2001, made one final screen appearance as Mr. Belvedere in 1997.

302. True or False: Darryl and Darryl never speak throughout the entire Newhart series.

299. True: The opening credits are actually outtakes from the movie On Golden Pond. At one point during the opening credits, you can clearly see Fonda and Hepburn in the car.

300. False: Willis filmed Die Hard while he was still starring in Moonlighting. The film immediately launched him into superstar status, which created some tension on the set of the television show. When Moonlighting began, Cybill Shepherd was regarded as the main star of the show; but as Willis's popularity grew, he became the audience favorite.

301. True: Hewitt guest starred on an episode of Ned and Stacey with Debra Messing and Thomas Haden Church, once again playing lovable Mr. Belvedere.

302. False: Darryl and Darryl are mostly silent, but in the final episode, they both shout "quiet!" to their chatty wives at the same time. This is the only time we ever hear them speak. In contrast with their spiritual successor Silent Bob, however, the actors themselves stayed quiet in public in real life as well.

303. Who sang the eponymous theme song for Moonlighting?

(A) Luther Vandross

(B) Al Green

(C) James Ingram

(D) Al Jarreau

304. Which baseball great did NOT make an appearance on the show Mr. Belvedere?

(A) Reggie Jackson

(B) Yogi Berra

(C) Mickey Mantle

(D) Willie Mays

305. True or False: Bruce Willis was the first and only actor to audition for the part of David Addison in Moonlighting.

303. D. The music for the song was written by Lee Holdridge, and Jarreau wrote the lyrics.

304. B. Jackson, Mantle, and Mays all guest starred in the first episode of the sixth season, along with Hank Aaron, Ernie Banks, Johnny Bench, and Harmon Killebrew. That's quite a lineup!

305. False: More than 2000 actors auditioned for the role. Willis auditioned somewhere in the middle of the pack, but show creator Glenn Gordon Caron knew he wanted Willis for the part as soon as he met him. The network, however, wasn't immediately convinced, and Caron was forced to wade through hundreds of other auditions before ABC finally gave him the go-ahead to hire Willis.

306. What year did beloved comedian Bob Newhart's sitcom Newhart premiere?

(A) 1980

(B) 1981

(C) 1982

(D) 1983

307. Where does Mr. Belvedere meet his future wife, Louise Gilbert?

(A) Grocery store

(B) Laundromat

(C) Bank

(D) Dry cleaners

308. Which actress had an uncredited appearance in one of the final episodes of Moonlighting as a woman in an elevator?

(A) Demi Moore

(B) Jodie Foster

(C) Elisabeth Shue

(D) Helen Hunt

306. C. Bob Newhart, known for his role as Dr. Robert Hartley on The Bob Newhart Show, returned to television in 1982's Newhart.

307. B. Mr. Belvedere bumps into Louise, a guest lecturer at the University of Pittsburgh, at the laundromat. They discover that they've both visited Africa, and this sparks an interest in continuing their conversation.

308. A. Moore, who didn't have a single line in the show, was married to Willis at the time. And in another nod to Willis, the actor is seen standing near a Die Hard poster in the same episode.

309. The sitcom Mr. Belvedere was based on the novel Belvedere by which author?

(A) Kenneth Roberts

(B) Gwen Davenport

(C) Alice Tilton

(D) Frank Richards

310. Which actor stars as Detective James Crockett in Miami Vice?

(A) Mickey Rourke

(B) Don Johnson

(C) Nick Nolte

(D) Jeff Bridges

311. How many seasons did Newhart run?

(A) 5

(B) 6

(C) 7

(D) 8

309. B. The novel was published in 1947, and it inspired three movies decades before the sitcom was created.

310. B. Although Rourke, Nolte, and Bridges were all considered for the part, ultimately it went to Johnson. The actor has also starred on the hit show Nash Bridges, and in movies like Tin Cup, The Other Woman, and Django Unchained.

311. D. After a shaky first and second season, Newhart hit its stride and aired until 1990.

312. True or False: Mr. Belvedere was almost cancelled after the third season.

313. Which song did Billy Joel write after being inspired by Moonlighting?

(A) "Big Man on Mulberry Street"

(B) "Uptown Girl"

(C) "The Longest Time"

(D) "Scenes from an Italian Restaurant"

314. True or False: American speed skating star Bonnie Blair won gold medals in three consecutive Olympic Games.

312. True: While the show was loved among viewers, it didn't bring in the ratings the network was hoping for. They decided to cancel it after the third season, but this caused such a fan uproar that they reconsidered. The show ended up airing for another three years!

313. A. Joel said he was inspired to write the song after watching Moonlighting, and then offered it to the producers to be used on the show. They used it in an episode aptly titled "Big Man on Mulberry Street."

314. True. Blair, who was inducted into the U.S. Olympic Hall of Fame in 2004, captured the 500 meters at the 1988 games. She then won both the 500 and 1,000 meters in 1992 and '94, finishing her career with five Olympic gold medals.